Steam Memories on Shed: 1950's – 1960's
No. 29: Edinburgh District Sheds

D Dunn

Copyright Book Law Publications 2012
ISBN 978-1-907094-85-9

INTRODUCTION

When the Scottish Region of British Railways adopted the former LMS shed code system in 1948, they followed the same path as all the other regions. However, whereas the North Eastern Region, for instance, contained within its boundaries those sheds which had once been LNER and North Eastern Railway beforehand – the former LMS sheds located in Yorkshire did not become part of the NE Region for some years afterwards – therefore requiring little in the way of change other than the creation of districts, the Scottish Region had to integrate sheds into districts which had once seen great rivalry and little in the way of co-operation. Such a situation existed in the '64' group of sheds which were based in Edinburgh with the headquarters or main shed at 64A St Margarets.

Within the '64' group two former LMS engine sheds were thrown into the mix, Dalry Road, and Carstairs. It made sense that the former depot was included because it was located firmly inside the city boundary of Edinburgh. Carstairs on the other hand was some distance away to the west and could easily have been included in the Glasgow '66' group (a transfer which eventually took place in June 1960 when Carstairs became 66E under Polmadie) rather than becoming 64D for twelve years.

The other depots within the '64' group included the former LNER sheds at Haymarket, Hawick, Polmont and Bathgate; a new establishment, fashioned from a former station was added from 1959 when Leith Central – 64H – was created to provide not only a depot for diesel multiple units, diesel shunters and occasional main-line locomotives, but also a place where driving and maintenance skills could be taught during the transition period from steam to diesel motive power.

We have brought together numerous pictures to illustrate all of these depots as they were throughout the formative years of BR. Hopefully, most if not all will be new to you therefore adding to your enjoyment.

(*Cover*) Peppercorn A1 No.60162 AULD REEKIE alongside the south wall of Haymarket shed on the last day of July 1955. *K.R.Pirt.*

(*Previous page*) Seen from the coal stage, the main running shed at St Margarets on Sunday 29th August 1965. This view is somewhat late in the day to show the true position on Sunday's of the past. The engine pits in the yard would not be visible for heavy metal, nor would the main line on the left. As for the yard on the right! Even the coaling stage road would have locomotives stabled sometimes. This, six-road, stone-built shed dated from 1866 and would just manage to make its century before the depot closed on 1st May 1967. However, what was original and what had been renewed is anyone's guess – it's a bit like Trigger's council broom! Already the diesels are muscling in; the Brush Type 4 could have arrived here from anywhere – they were profusely spread around the country with every region having some by this date. As for the steam locomotives, they are identified as follows, left to right: B1 No.61344, V2 No.60955, Std. Cl.4 No.80026, B1 No.61099, and, on the south side of the shed, in the yard beyond the sand furnace, another BR Std. Cl.4 No.80114. *A.R.Thompson.*

Printed and bound by The Amadeus Press, Cleckheaton, West Yorkshire
First published in the United Kingdom by Book Law Publications, 382 Carlton Hill, Nottingham, NG4 1JA

64A ST MARGARETS

The back door of St Margarets depot with resident V1 No.67609 standing sentry. This was the road vehicle entrance to the depot with looming tenements overlooking the proceedings in the yard. For those who lived in those blocks, life must have been intolerable at times. Although undated, this scene was probably captured in 1952, after the V1 had attended main works at Darlington for a major overhaul. In October 1953, during the 2-6-2Ts next General overhaul, it was converted to Class V3. *C.J.B.Sanderson.*

(*previous page*) The 70ft turntable at St Margarets was installed in 1942 on part of the site previously occupied by a square roundhouse which had been built by the North British Railway for the North Eastern in 1871; the NBR took over the building in 1902 with the NER renting space on a 'per locomotive' basis. The cramped site containing St Margarets engine shed offered few opportunities for enlargement of the depot or the installation of modern appliances. The turntable and the additional siding space, which the demolition of the roundhouse offered, served the depot for a quarter of a century up to closure, as did the ancient 300 ft. long coaling stage (much rebuilt by BR days) which must have been one of the busiest single-sided stages in the country. Gresley A4 No.60019 BITTERN only spent thirteen days allocated to St Margarets shed during October and November 1963. In that time it was captured on film leaving the coaling stage and proceeding onto the turntable prior to visiting the ash pit. Note the build-up of grime on the top of the streamlined casing courtesy of eighteen months of not being cleaned at Gateshead shed! The Pacific moved on to Ferryhill from where it worked for nearly three more years before becoming one of the last two operational A4s – KINGFISHER was the other – both withdrawn on 5th September 1966. *I.W.Coulson.*

Resident J38 No.65915 stables alongside the single road repair shop on 22nd September 1962. The modern brickwork shows the age of this building, circa 1943, as part of the wartime re-modelling of the depot's track layout and facilities in 1942/43. The well equipped and spacious repair building adjoined the engine shed. *A.Ives.*

Looking west in 1961 at the shed entrance/exit tracks from the south (main) running shed where they join the main line by London Road bridge, opposite the controlling signal box known simply as ST MARGARETS. *C.J.B.Sanderson.*

The old 1846-vintage roundhouse, or what was left of it, located on the north side of the main line at St Margarets. Surrounded on its west, north and eastern boundaries by the remnants of the former locomotive works, the roundhouse had no room for expansion. Its original small diameter turntable could serve only shunting tanks during the latter decades of its existence. A disastrous fire during LNER days had destroyed the circular stone building which protected this site but the stalls were untouched during the conflagration and were thereafter used to stable many of the depot's allocation of forty-odd tank engines. In this view captured on 21st April 1956 from, it appears the signal box, Y9 0-4-0STs and 0-6-0T dominate the 'shed' with its fourteen available stalls. In latter years diesel shunters would take the place of many of these steam locomotives. *C.J.B.Sanderson.*

C16 No.67492 sits comfortably in its stall 'inside' the roundhouse during the early evening of Wednesday 31st July 1957. The engine is in steam and appears to have 'nipped' on shed for a quick change or examination of its front left buffer which has been removed, allowing us to see the wooden pad which cushioned the buffer from its beam! We are looking south-east across the main line towards the coaling stage, the end of which is visible. The ever present Y9 class is represented by No.68102 which is complete with its coal carrier. *I.Falcus.*

The outside roundhouse with its fourteen or so stabling roads was also useful during the diesel era when the likes of these North British Loco. Co., built 0-4-0 diesel-hydraulics were kept away from the steam shed across the main line. Not that the segregation on grounds of cleanliness was of any consequence because most of these shunters were made redundant virtually when purchased by BR. The yards and goods facilities, which their steam counterparts had worked for decades, were closing at an alarming rate and many of these little diesels were condemned long before their tenth birthdays, one of the youngest to go was less than seven years old! *C.J.B.Sanderson.*

The London Road side of the old roundhouse on the morning of Monday 30th May 1955 with Y9 No.68099, complete with coal carrier, J88 No.68354 and another larger but unidentified J83 tank engine sharing the same stall. The 0-4-0ST, which was withdrawn in November 1956, worked the whole of its life from St Margarets where, in the adjacent workshops, this class usually had their major overhauls carried out. To the left of the locomotives stand a major proportion of 64A's miniature snowplough allocation of which none would be fitted to any of this trio. *F.W.Hampson.*

The offices and stores buildings on Clockmill Road form the background for this aspect of the roundhouse on Saturday 24th April 1954 with two J88 Nos.68338 and 68325 stabled for the weekend. Note the former LMS type of power classification on the bunker, above the number – 0FT; the route availability R.A.3 gave these engines a wide range over most BR lines. When British Railways took over the shed had seven of this class allocated but that rose by one more in a couple of years. However, as the diesels began to arrive the J88 numbers at St Margarets dropped to just four in 1959 until there was none! Tucked away on the left is Y9 No.68119. *C.J.B.Sanderson.*

The well-worn and continually used sleeper-built pathway which linked the two halves of St Margarets shed separated by the main line. On Sunday 28th July 1957 stabled K2 No.61775 LOCH TREIG leaves sufficient room for the comings and goings of the staff. *D.Fairley.*

The final Peppercorn A2 No.60539 BRONZINO stands amongst the ash and clinker surrounding the ash pits. The sunken wagon road designed to make the disposal of the waste easier for shed staff is located between the two ash pit roads. Strategically placed water taps and associated hoses were provided to douse the hot piles whilst at the same time prevent any conflagration inside the wooden bodied wagons. The date is 30th September 1961 and the Heaton based Pacific is showing external signs of neglect which was not unusual by this date especially for locomotives allocated to sheds on Tyneside. The day following the taking of this photograph, No.60539 was transferred to Tweedmouth to act out its final year of operation as main-line pilot. Obviously before it goes south again it will have to be turned unless a job to Dundee, Aberdeen or points west of Edinburgh beckoned, or more than likely the path taken to pick-up a southbound freight from Leith would see the use being made of local junctions to point the engine in the correct direction. *C.J.B.Sanderson.*

On that same Saturday in September 1961, another Tweedmouth engine is facing the wrong way for working home. Perhaps the same circumstances surrounding the A2s departure also applied to K3 No.61969, which is being tended to by its driver. *C.J.B.Sanderson.*

The ubiquitous Stanier Class 5, a class which probably more than any other – barring the WD 2-8-0 – managed to get virtually everywhere. This specimen resided at St Margarets on 9th May 1964 and was allocated to Aberdeen's Ferryhill shed but its route to Edinburgh is unknown. Was it via Perth or Dundee and the Tay bridge? The holes to accept the fixings for snow plough brackets can be seen in the bufferbeam. *C.J.B.Sanderson.*

Sunday 16th August 1964 presented a rather cramped yard to any visitors. Resident B1 No.61345 simmers amongst friends whilst one of the erstwhile Clayton Type 1s may well be wondering where it all went wrong! *C.J.B.Sanderson.*

Compared with many of the larger depots located along the ECML, few Pacifics were allocated to St Margarets in BR days, and most of those that were, arrived during the final years of the depot's life. A handful of A4s even managed short terms at 64A, most of that time in store at other locations, but No.60001 SIR RONALD MATTHEWS was not one of them. This 16th August 1964 view across the ash pits reveals that the Gateshead Pacific is turned and ready for a dash south, although the glory days of the ECML steam hauled expresses are all but finished by now. The 'Deltic' diesels had become the new champions of the Running Department and most of the Gresley thoroughbreds were either condemned or in storage by August 64'. *C.J.B.Sanderson.*

A proper shunting engine: N15 No.69148 reveals its sixty tons of prime shunting prowess on its day off at St Margarets on Sunday 12th July 1953. These tanks could stable either on this side of the main line in the straight shed or on one of the former roundhouse stalls on the north side of the line where they towered over the adjacent Y9s. *C.J.B.Sanderson.*

64B HAYMARKET

Colwick K2 No.61773 prepares to work back to Glasgow whilst undergoing running-in trials from Cowlairs on Monday 29th September 1952 following a General overhaul. It was to be the following Saturday before Cowlairs were satisfied that the 2-6-0 was ready to return to traffic at 38A. Haymarket's 70ft turntable, which was situated at the east end of the shed, had plenty of room to spare for the K2. *C.J.B.Sanderson.*

During the A.S.L.E.F. strike of 1955 (29th May to 14th June) BR had a problem with the stabling of locomotives which are not normally all 'put to bed' at the same time. The engine sheds were bulging and every available, and suitable, stretch of siding was employed to 'park' the dead locomotives. This is the main line alongside Haymarket engine shed on 30th May 1955 with a gang of enthusiasts taking advantage of the 'engines being at home' and there not being any traffic on the main line. Note the A3 on the right which is actually in steam. The line-up here, of which unfortunately we have no record except for a couple of the photographed locomotives, included B1s, D11/2s, K3, A1s, with Nos.61355 and 62677 identified. Note that all the tenders are topped-up ready for the eventual return to traffic. *F.W.Hampson.*

Eastfield B1 No.61140 makes a pleasing sight outside the west end of the shed on Saturday 2nd February 1957. Although slightly stained, the paintwork still shows that ex-works finish from one week beforehand when the B1 was released from Cowlairs after a General overhaul which had begun on the previous Christmas Eve. The coal weighing tender coupled to 61140 had started life as a conventional tender behind No.(6)1229 on 2nd September 1947 but on 11th December 1951 the tender began a rebuild which saw it converted. Its first coupling was to No.61140 from 9th April to 9th July 1952. It then went to No.61172 from 15th August to 12th September 1952 when, at Cowlairs, it was detached and then coupled to a waiting No.61140 again. The Eastfield B1 remained coupled to the tender for the rest of its life until being sold for scrap in February 1967. Looking at the headboard with what appears to be No.71 pasted on, just, the 4-6-0 has probably worked into Edinburgh with a football supporters' special. *C.J.B.Sanderson.*

This view of A4 No.60011 EMPIRE OF INDIA, alongside the south wall of the shed on Saturday 20th April 1957, gives us a glimpse of the rather ornate brickwork employed at Haymarket. Built in 1894, the eight-road shed replaced a cramped three-road establishment which was located further to the east, near Haymarket passenger station. As is well known, 64B looked after all of the ECML Pacifics allocated to the Edinburgh district, amongst them the Gresley A4s. Note the driver obliging the photographer with a blast on the chime whistle, probably one of the most memorable sounds of all the whistles fitted to British steam locomotives. *C.J.B.Sanderson.*

A selection of headboards outside the stores at Haymarket shed in October 1957. *C.J.B.Sanderson.*

72002 CLAN CAMPBELL at Haymarket in August 1957. By now the Pacific was wearing a 64B shedplate and was working over the Waverley route as far as Carlisle. This 'Clan' was joined by others at Haymarket in October as follows: No.72000, 72005 and 72006. Rumours had it that the class was not popular at either Polmadie or Haymarket. In April 1958 the four at 64B returned to 66A but our photographic subject made a return visit to Haymarket in November 1959 when No.72001 arrived in Edinburgh for the first time. No.72000 came back too but instead went to St Margarets and was joined for the first time by Nos.72003 and 72004. Working once again over the ECML and Waverley routes did nothing to endear the class to the Edinburgh men and by the following March all five were back in Glasgow! Gresley, it seems, had made a lasting impression on those former LNER locomen. *C.J.B.Sanderson.*

During the period when the shed was undergoing alteration to accommodate the coming diesel fleet at Haymarket, steam operations continued almost undisturbed. In this illustration from Saturday 29th August 1959, Peppercorn A2 No.60535 HORNETS BEAUTY prepares to go off shed to haul an afternoon southbound working whilst other steam locomotives are stabled inside the building. Meanwhile, evidence of the roof demolition can be seen through the gap at the rear of the A2s tender. *C.J.B.Sanderson.*

The ex-LMS presence in Edinburgh was not confined to the likes of Dalry Road and St Margarets sheds. Haymarket too was subject to visitors from near and far. In 1959 for reasons as yet unexplained, Kingmoor 'Jubilee' No.45729 FURIOUS made a visit to 64B and is seen backing onto the shed after replenishing its tender. *C.J.B.Sanderson.*

The purists might disagree about the worthiness of this picture for inclusion but this compiler thinks that it shows the steam locomotive in one of its better poses, courtesy of shadows and light. It is late evening on 30th September 1961 as resident A3 No.60096 PAPYRUS gets ready to reverse on shed after filling its tender at the coaling plant. The sun is setting and a stiff breeze is building from the west – change is on the way! This former master of ECML passenger express workings had only been back at Haymarket for a week since return from Doncaster 'Plant' works where it received not just its last 'General' overhaul but also its final works repair. During the following December No.60096 would be transferred to St Margarets, in effect evicted from Haymarket as surplus to requirements. In September 1963, straight after the cessation of the summer timetable, the Pacific was condemned and later sold for scrap. Past glories were simply that – past! *C.J.B.Sanderson.*

One of the new ECML race horses – 'Deltic' D9016 is stabled outside the north-east corner of the shed in 1962. *C.J.B.Sanderson.*

64C DALRY ROAD

A general view of a section of the Dalry Road (64C) shed site looking due north from the steps leading from Dundee Street on Saturday 1st June 1963. McIntosh Caledonian 3F 0-6-0 No.57565 steals the limelight but as can be seen it is certainly not in service having been withdrawn during the previous January; a one-way trip to Inverurie works and oblivion beckoned. Besides the shed plate still being in situ, note the large lump of coal nestling on the cab roof, effectively holding the weather sheet in place. Fairburn Cl.4 tank No.42168 hiding behind, is simply stabled and would remain operational until the following March when it too was condemned. The 2-6-4T was a relative newcomer to 64C having transferred from St Margarets in May 1962. Since being put into traffic in October 1948, the Cl.4 tank had worked the whole of its life in Scotland, covering a good part of the geography during its fifteen year life. Starting at Polmadie, it managed to serve just 'A' sheds until its arrival here; Perth, and Inverness became home in December 1954 and March 1960 respectively prior to its transfer to 64A. Beyond is the two-road, timber built, repair shop which pre-dated the 1911-built engine shed and was once an operational engine shed prior to 1895. Part of the 1911 shed can be seen in the background with two Stanier 5s, Nos.45023 and 45476, alongside. The eagle-eyed will have spotted, on the extreme right, a 350 h.p. 0-6-0DE shunter parked on the coaling stage ramp. *C.J.B.Sanderson.*

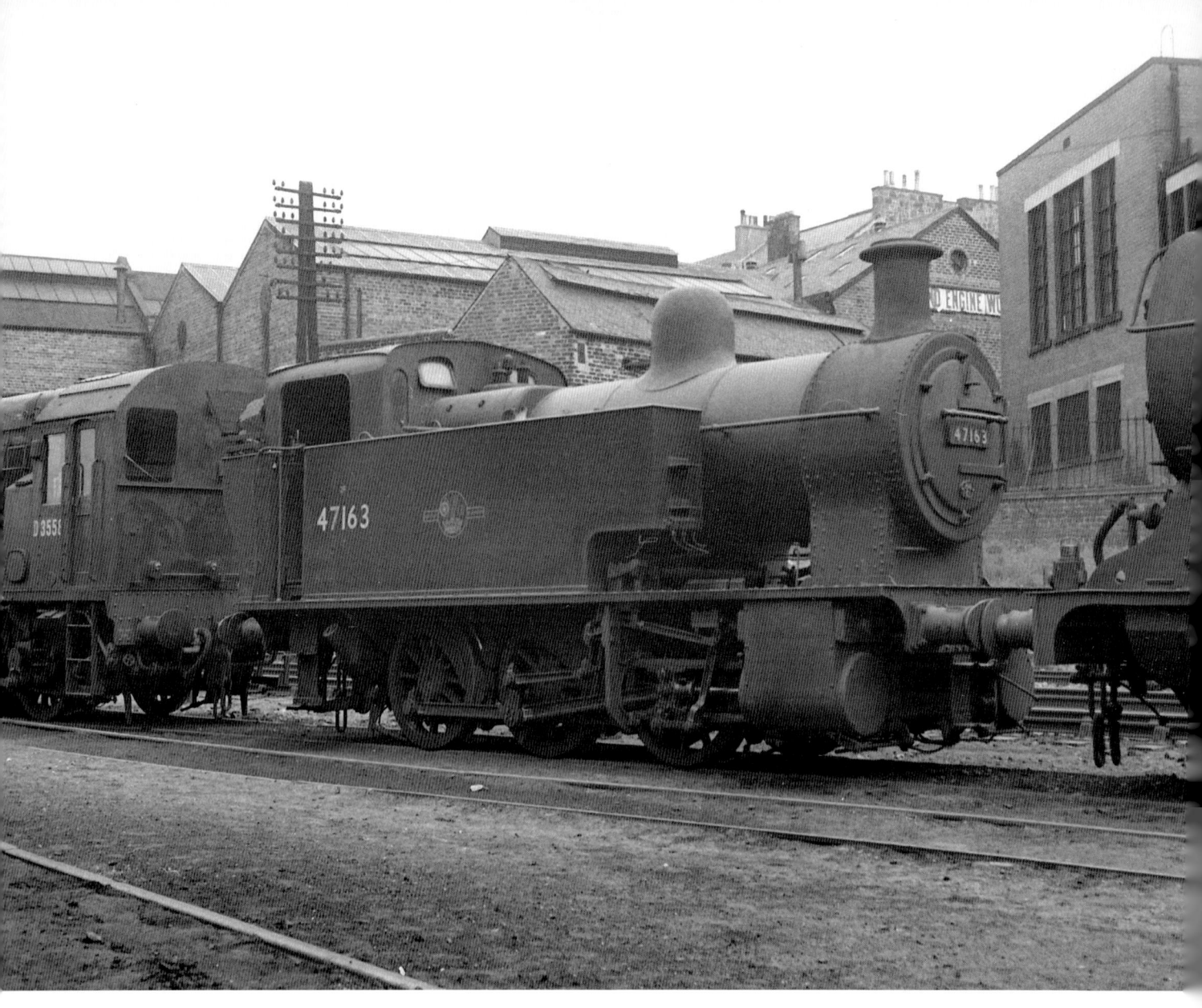

Dalry Road's allocation for much of the BR era was blessed with one of the ten LMS 1928-built 2F 0-6-0 'Dock Tanks' in the shape of No.47163. Sister No.47162, was also on the books until shortly after Nationalisation when it was transferred to St Margarets. Three others were based at Greenock whilst the remaining five all worked from appropriately located sheds in England. No.47163 worked the Balerno branch whilst at Dalry Road, a duty it shared with No.47162 until the latter's move to 64A. The date of this photograph is 17th May 1959 and one of the diesel shunters which encroached on the branch work, D3558, and then took over from the 0-6-0T, stands behind No.47163. *I.W.Coulson.*

Just before Nationalisation, Dalry Road received six nearly new, Derby-built, Fairburn tank locomotives which had arrived via Hamilton, 66C or 27C to give that shed its final LMS coding. The numbers of the engines at that time were: 2268, 2269, 2270, 2271, 2272, and 2273 – a 'running flush' of sorts. More importantly, these 2-6-4T were renown for their reliability and crew comfort, just what the shed required. During the Fifties' Dalry Road lost four of these tanks so that by 1960 only two of the original half dozen remained – 42272 and 42273. The latter left 64C when the shed was closed in October 1965; it didn't have far to go, just down the line to St Margarets. However, No.42272, seen at Dalry Road on 1st June 1963, was withdrawn during December 1962 and languished on the 'dead line' awaiting the call to the breakers. *C.J.B.Sanderson.*

Despite appearances, the former LNER contingent of the Scottish Region hadn't taken over at Dalry Road completely by Sunday 20th October 1963. The rather grotty looking Gresley A3 No.60052 PRINCE PALATINE, hidden in part by the morning shadows cast by a low sun, was one of the St Margarets charges and was stabled for the weekend due to the usual lack of space at 64A. This particular Pacific became the last active A3 and managed to survive in traffic until January 1966, effectively outliving its weekend retreat by some months. The respectable looking Thompson B1 behind is apparently No.61245 MURRAY OF ELIBANK, one of five B1s which would transfer to Dalry Road shed for the final few years before closure in October 1965. The substantial brick-built, four-road engine shed turned out to have been a compromise and was erected on the site of a previous shed, within an already cramped site. A planned ten-road shed, which was to be built at Slateford Junction circa 1899 never materialised for various reasons whilst another ear-marked site, on the outskirts of Edinburgh, was opposed by the NBR who objected to a necessary new bridge being erected over their line! *C.J.B.Sanderson.*

Two old-timers visit the shed on 3rd September 1959 during a period when they were heading railtours all over the Region. Ex-CR 4-2-2 Single No.123, of 1886, in glorious blue, and former North British 'Glen' 4-4-0 No.256 GLEN DOUGLAS, of 1913, were coupled together in a marriage of convenience alongside the repair shop; it was never like this pre-Grouping in Edinburgh! *C.J.B.Sanderson.*

Unlike the Stanier Class 5s, which were often found allocated to ex-North British/LNER sheds; Eastfield, St Margarets, Fort William, etc., amongst them; the Hughes/Fowler 'Crab' allocated to the Scottish Region rarely strayed from their native former LMS establishments for some reason. Dalry Road maintained at least a brace of the class for many years – some eleven different engines had resided here at one time or another – but by the mid-1950s their numbers fell away so that a single member represented the class by the end of the decade. That sole example was No.42807, seen in the yard on the south side of the shed on 21st May 1956. The 2-6-0 had transferred from Kingmoor to Dalry Road during World War Two, only its second move! In March 1961 No.42807 transferred away to Ayr and 64C's link with the class was severed. *F.W.Hampson.*

Two long serving members of the depot's BR allocation, Stanier Cl.5s Nos.45022 and 45023 are caught together on film in the shed yard during 1962. These two were amongst the oldest of the class having been put into traffic at Perth North in August 1934 to work the Highland line trains to Inverness. Transferring to Dalry Road shed in January 1950, from different depots, they certainly proved their mixed traffic credentials by working passenger services one day and coal trains the next. Both were withdrawn in September 1963, their places taken by other Stanier 5s. Despite working separately for much of their lives – both engines left Scotland in September 1935 and worked from a variety of English depots in all corners of the former LMS system – they came together at what proved to be their final shed, ironically in Scotland. *C.J.B.Sanderson.*

64D CARSTAIRS

The four-road engine shed at Carstairs originated in the 1850s when the junction here became an important locomotive changing point. Rebuilding took place in the mid 1930s with a mechanical coaling plant replacing the coal stage, and the shed itself virtually renewed, albeit with lightweight materials which reflected the paucity of the financial budgets of the period, even with Government help. By June 1962, when this view of BR-built Cl.4 No.42177 was recorded, the cladding on the shed roof and the smoke vents had deteriorated sufficiently to require further renewal; that however never took place during steam days and this is the condition in which the shed faced closure in February 1967. Diesels used the building for a number of years afterwards, some kind of re-cladding having taken place after 1967. Nothing remains of this place now except the passenger station. *C.J.B.Sanderson.*

In June 1960 Carstairs shed was recoded 66E under the authority now of Polmadie – it's perhaps rightful placing in the great scheme of Scottish engine shed grouping. Resident Stanier Cl.5 No.44952 stables at the east end of the shed, adjacent to the repair shop, on 28th April 1963 sporting what every locomotive on BR, other than ex-works specimens, now wore, a heavy coat of grime. This engine was LMS built and started life at Crewe North shed in March 1946; in March 1948 it was transferred to Carstairs where it remained to the end, virtually; it was condemned in October 1966 as steam motive power was being wound down in Scottish Region. *C.J.B.Sanderson.*

The batch of five Scottish Region based (66A – Polmadie) 'Clans' were all withdrawn in December 1962 but those five allocated to 12A Kingmoor (72005-72009) thrived for a few more years until they too were condemned. On 9th June 1962, when the class was still intact, Kingmoor's No.72008 CLAN MACLEOD, has its fire cleaned over the Carstairs ash pits, and is ready for a southbound working. The ash facilities here were installed during the depot's rebuild in 1934/5. Always an untidy area at any steam depot, this section was dirty, and dangerous too for the unwary. This 'Clan' lasted until April 1966 when it was withdrawn at Kingmoor. Its final journey brought it once again to Carstairs but that event saw it pass through, being hauled 'dead' to a scrapyard in Shettleston. *C.J.B.Sanderson.*

Besides all the LMS and BR Standard classes which resided and visited this place during the latter period of the Fifties', it must be remembered that nearly two-thirds of the depots' complement of approximately fifty locomotives in 1948 consisted former Caledonian types such as this long-time resident Cl.3P 4-4-0 No.54505, seen on Saturday 19th May 1956. As British Railways came into being, Carstairs had nine of these capable locomotives on their strength, along with twice as many 0-6-0 tender engines. However, only one 0-4-4T was resident for much of the BR era, LMS-built CR 2P No.55261 which was just poking into the picture from the right. *F.W.Hampson.*

Carstairs was home to two of the Scottish Region based WD Austerity 2-10-0s for the whole of their BR service. No.90753, as WD No.73777 arrived from Ashford works, after a post-war refurbishment, on 7th February 1949, complete with air pumps and W^D markings on its tender sides; it worked from 64D until withdrawn on 6th July 1961. Two days after No.90753's arrival, No.90768, as No.73792 and in a similar condition, came onto the property after a Light overhaul provided by the Southern Region works at Ashford in late 1948. For its first major overhaul, No.73792 entered Cowlairs works on 25th January 1950 and after a prolonged Heavy General emerged as BR No.90768 on 17th June 1950. This illustration shows the exhibition standard finish after that Cowlairs HG. Now, Cowlairs turned out most of its repaired engines in black paint but this particular 2-10-0 was actually destined for an exhibition at Dunfermline, hence the immaculate black livery and burnished metalwork! Note that a cast front numberplate was yet to be fitted but the 'stand-in' painted numbers have been applied to an excellent standard. The shedplate is simply black and is virtually invisible with no white paint to pick out the 64D (LMS-style shed plates were still new to the former NBR/LNER workshop) however, in true Cowlairs style the locomotive's home shed name has been painted on the front bufferbeam. The star around the smokebox fastening spindle was not unique to 90768; 90761 had one too until October 1961 at least. Perhaps it was the same one as worn by 90768 which appears to have lost its embellishment during the 1950s. You will probably never see a picture of a BR owned WD 2-10-0 looking so smart – ever! No.90768 worked from Carstairs shed until withdrawn on 30th July 1962, although it had been laid-up since the previous summer (see later). It was cut up at Darlington works during November 1963. *C.J.B.Sanderson.*

Part of the Carstairs breakdown train contained this former Caledonian Railway six-wheel passenger vehicle (M.354750) which had been suitably converted. This illustration, from 10th July 1950, shows the van stabled in front of the depot's office block. By 1960 this van, and indeed the whole breakdown train – including a similar vehicle to this, the adjacent packing van, an open wagon, and the crane itself (a 1907-built Cravens 20-ton appliance numbered RS1053 in the LMS fleet, which had come from Perth in 1943) – had been withdrawn in favour of a pair of 'newer' eight-wheel, bogie vehicles, complete with jacks but sans crane. *C.J.B.Sanderson.*

This was a familiar sight to all who visited Carstairs in the early Sixties'. A long row of stored, and condemned locomotives which were stabled in sidings on the southern boundary of the depot. Featured are three former Carstairs engines: 0-4-4T No.55261, 0-6-0 No.57451, and WD 2-10-0 No.90768 which present a sorry sight as they await the call to the breakers on 24th September 1961. *I.W.Coulson.*

64E POLMONT

64E Polmont was located in Linlithgow, virtually due north of its county neighbour and fellow ex-NBR shed at Bathgate. A transverse pitched roof spanned the five roads of the building using a design which was employed by both the North British and Caledonian railways for many of their engine sheds. The shed was open at both ends which effectively allowed more stabling room on a longer yard. Not immediately apparent from this distance is the timber construction used throughout the structure, albeit with a slated roof, which was erected in 1914 and opened immediately after the New Year celebrations for 1915. Why timber was chosen is unknown but various factors must be considered; a financial reason was probably the strongest candidate but mining subsidence could also have been in the minds of the surveyors when the site was chosen. This shed had replaced another earlier three-road shed located at Bo'ness junction and known as Manuel. Ironically, the timber-built engine shed at Polmont shed stood the test of time and remained intact up to closure nearly fifty years later in May 1964. This view was recorded on 27th June 1948 which, as can be seen, was a Sunday with the locomotive stud at home. *K.H.Cockerill.*

Another aspect of the shed from the east but at a slightly later date – 15th August 1954, another Sunday and another dull summer day! *F.W.Hampson.*

This Y9 must have been the pride of Polmont shed judging by its external condition but that was not quite the case. No.68113 was photographed on 24th May 1952 just six weeks after completing a Heavy Intermediate overhaul at Cowlairs. However, the cleanliness is certainly worthy of comment. Besides its couple of dozen or so 0-6-0 tender engines from classes J35, J36, J37 and J38, Polmont also had a dozen or more shunting engines when BR inherited the depot. Most were six-coupled tanks from classes J83, J88 and the former Great Eastern J69, along with a trio of N15 but complimenting those were a couple of these 0-4-0ST – 68104 and 68113 – which had been at the shed since its opening. No.68104 transferred to Kipps in November 1960 and never came back. No.68113, which was loyal to Polmont throughout its life except for four days in May 1955 when it was sent to St Margarets, was condemned in late January 1958 when a diesel shunter took over its work. A third Y9, which became No.68108, had also been at the depot from opening but had moved on to Bathgate in March 1940. Others came for short periods and moved on. What they all had in common and which is illustrated here by No.68113, is the fact that none required the distinctive four-wheel coal carrier which other class members (see St Margarets in particular) needed for their daily work. The Polmont Y9s worked at Falkirk (High) and Camelon where supplies of coal were to hand. *C.J.B.Sanderson.*

One of Polmont's trio of J69 orphans from the GE Section, No.68524, outside the west end of the shed on 15th August 1954. This 0-6-0T arrived at Polmont from Parkeston in September 1928 as LNER No.7347. Accompanying it was No.7368 (68544) which had come from Stratford. In September 1943 they were joined by No.7356 (68533) which had originally transferred to St Margarets in 1928 and then gradually worked across to Polmont via Dunfermline, Thornton Junction and Eastfield. By the date of the photograph No.68533 had been withdrawn; next would be No.68544 on the last day of January 1955. No.68524 must have had a charmed life because it was working until June 1959 before it too was taken to Cowlairs and broken up. Note the shunters' step and horizontal handrail on the bunker; fitments put on at Cowlairs in 1928 following NBR shunting practice. *F.W.Hampson.*

Another of the dumb-buffered engines built by the North British Railway were those 0-6-0T of J88 class. No.68324, still showing its previous owners' LNER identity, is standing in the shed yard on 21st July 1951. One of three J88 allocated to Polmont at this time – 68350 and 68354 were the others – No.68324 was the first to leave the shed; it was withdrawn in July 1958. *C.J.B.Sanderson.*

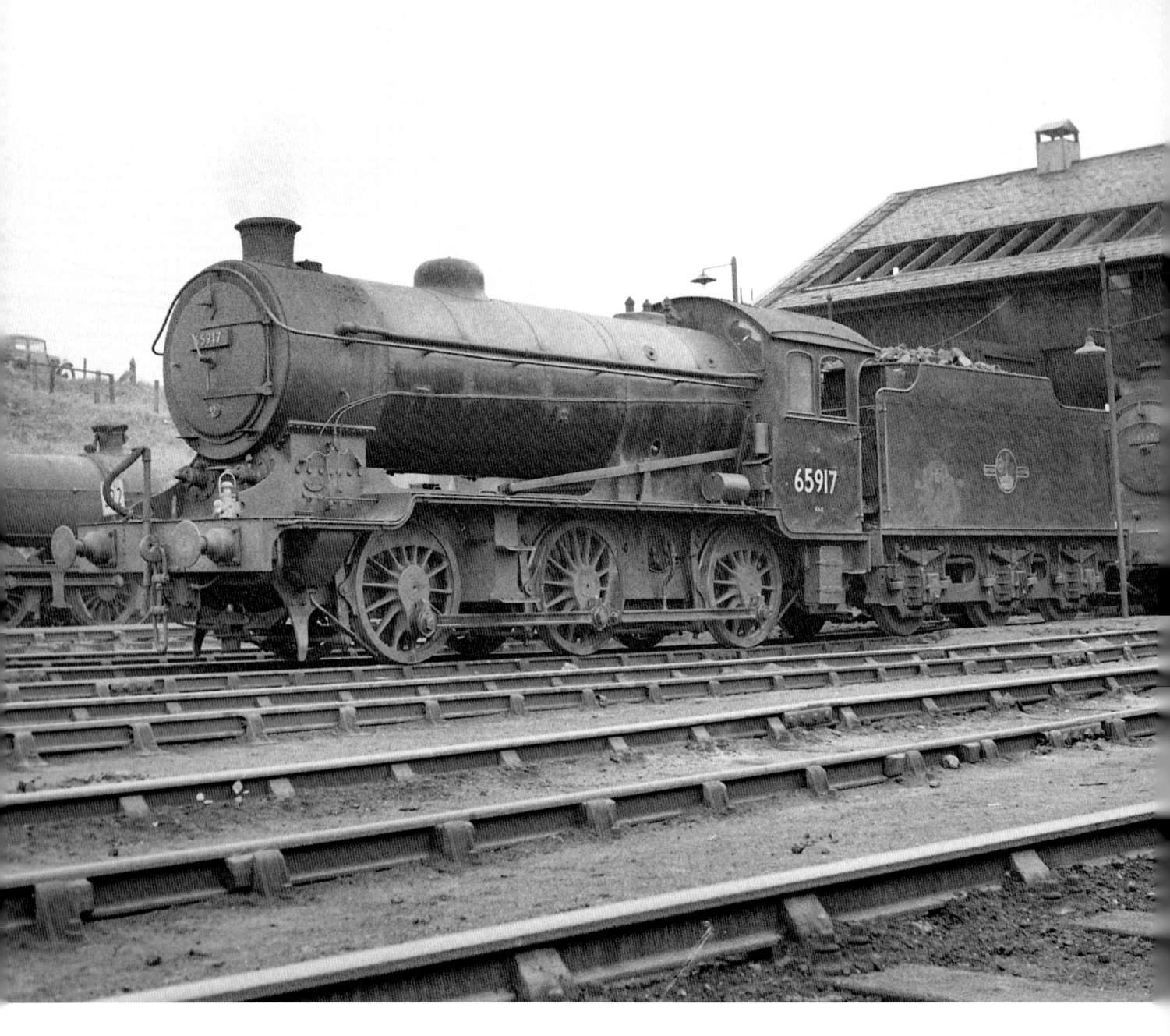

Resident J38 No.65917 shares a quiet shed yard with other 0-6-0s in 1961. The glass in the shed roof has now been removed, decline has set in but it would be another three years before the depot was closed. *A.R.Thompson.*

Besides the for LNER classes allocated to Polmont in BR days, the shed also acquired a pair of new Doncaster built Ivatt Cl.4s in August 1951, Nos.43140 and 43141. These 'ugly ducklings' supplemented the duties carried out by the depot's J37s over the longer distance mineral workings. Eastfield shed in Glasgow was also blessed with a handful of these useful 2-6-0s but their batch had been built at Horwich – BR was certainly acting as one company now even though local traditions were firmly embedded in the pre-Group period. This is Eastfield's No.43135 paying a visit to Polmont on Saturday 24th May 1952. Whatever the Polmont enginemen thought of these engines is unknown but the Cl.4s remained at 64E until June 1958 in the case of No.43141 which then moved to Hawick. Sister No.43140 went to Grangemouth in March of the following year. Their transfers had nothing to do with local acceptance and more to do with traffic loss at Polmont. In the decade since BR took over, the allocation had virtually halved in numbers. Along with the Eastfield contingent, the former Ivatt twins from Polmont moved away from Scottish Region in September 1963 to work out the rest of their lives on the North Eastern Region. *C.J.B.Sanderson.*

On 17th May 1959 this melancholy line of four 'Scottish Directors' was photographed at Polmont. From left to right the D11/2s were: Nos.62682 HAYSTOUN OF BUCKLAW, 62673 EVAN DHU, 62683 HOBBIE ELLIOTT, and 62694 JAMES FITZJAMES. Although none had worked for sometime, a couple of years in some cases, only one had been condemned and of the three 'in store' none had the statutory chimney covering! Both Eastfield and Haymarket sheds were responsible for this mini dump, in equal measures. None of the 4-4-0s would work again and none would return to their home depots. The engines' fortunes would take them to different venues for scrapping: No.62673, ex Eastfield, was condemned in July 1959 and went to Cowlairs for breaking up. No.62682, also a former 65A charge, was not withdrawn until July 1961 after which it went to Inverurie for cutting up. No.62683 was at Haymarket until arriving here and it had been condemned during the previous September and would shortly be departing for Kilmarnock. Finally No.62694 another Haymarket engine which was condemned in November 1959 and then sold for scrap to Arnott Young at Old Kirkpatrick. Dumps such as this were appearing all over the country and some of the Scottish Region locations one in particular and not far from here at Bo'ness, became one of the biggest dumps attracting enthusiasts from all over Britain during its period of notoriety. *F.W.Hampson.*

Polmont's first diesel locomotive was a North British built 200 h.p. 0-4-0 shunter numbered 11707 (D2707) which arrived at 64E on 20th October 1956 and worked locally until moving on to Dunfermline on 2nd November 1957. This is the said locomotive on Saturday 20th April 1957 returning from a shunting job complete with brake van and enclosed guards. Note the two-man operation for the diesel! When 11707 left for 62C, it was immediately replaced with another member of the same class 11703 (2703) which remained at Polmont until moving on to Grangemouth at the closure of the shed in May 1964. During that time the depot was fortunate to have the services of the following diesels from new: D3557, D3558 and D3559 which all arrived on 15th November 1958. All three, except D3558, worked at 64E until 11th January 1964 when nearby Grangemouth took over their care; D3558 had moved on to St Margarets in September 1959 as surplus to Polmont's requirements. In 1960 0-4-0DHs D2776 (31st October), D2777 (21st November), and D2778 (28th November), arrived and took over some of the depot's lighter work. Once again, the first and last of the batch stayed to the end before moving to 65F in January 64' whilst the middle member of the batch had transferred to Kipps during the month ending 8th September 1962. Two other 350 h.p. 0-6-0DE shunters came on transfer but remained to the end; D3409 was ex Kipps and an exchange for D2777 in 1962. D3556 came much earlier from Bathgate in December 1958. So the history of Polmont's 'diesel years' are somewhat brief but then so was the life of the depot in relation to others. Not quite fifty years, start to finish! Perhaps the man who came up with the timber shed idea was right after all. *C.J.B.Sanderson.*

64F BATHGATE

Another of the 64 District depots located in Linlithgow, 64F Bathgate, with a 'full house' on Sunday 29th May 1949. The shed building, also consisting a transverse pitched roof, similar to Polmont, spanned the six stabling roads. The roof appears fairly intact in this 1949 view from the east end of the yard. Bathgate shed opened in 1902 and replaced a two-road structure built by the Edinburgh & Bathgate Railway in 1849 and which stood nearby. Unlike Polmont, Bathgate was of a more substantial construction with brick walls. Being that the business of the depot was the movement of coal, the allocation in 1949 consisted almost entirely of 0-6-0 tender engines, although half a dozen 0-6-2T and a trio of 4-4-0s, all from different classes, also graced the yard. This morning view illustrates nicely the typical allocation of engines found here at that time but things were to change during the next decade. *K.H.Corkerill.*

Viewed from a point adjacent to the coal stage, actually the cab roof of the second locomotive featured in the following illustration, the equipment used by contractors to rebuild the engine shed in 1953-54 can be clearly seen dominating the shed yard in 1953; the requirement of such a crane will be become apparent. During the time that the roof was being removed and replaced, resident locomotives were stabled in any available space on the yard. The location of this depot in the midst of the central belt coalfield is evidenced by the mounds of colliery waste in the distance. The proximity of underground workings played havoc with the infrastructure of the depot and subsidence was a continual problem especially regarding the coaling stage and, as can be seen, the shed building itself. On the right, full of wagons on this date, the slightly elevated siding would soon become a dumping ground for redundant locomotives from not only Bathgate but other sheds too. *K.H.Cockerill.*

The carrying of destination boards atop locomotive smokebox doors had been the practice on the former North British lines since before Grouping and although it had ceased during the conflict of 1939-45, it was regenerated post-war. This is D34 No.62495 GLEN LUSS displaying a BATHGATE board at Bathgate shed in 1953, during the period of the shed rebuilding. In true Cowlairs style, the class of the engine and the name of the home shed have been carefully painted on the bufferbeam. Note that the tender is still adorned with LNER albeit under a coating of grime. *K.H.Cockerill.*

Looking as though it has not been used for a while, C15 No.67473 is stabled inside the near-completed shed on 15th August 1954. Above, the roof is supported by some rather substantial girders whilst at rail level the contractors are still at work creating the concrete pits for the running roads. A petrol-engined powered hopper, used for carrying building materials, stands on its own temporary railway allowing reasonable quantities of concrete to be delivered to the internal working area from an outside supply. Note the, as yet, virtually unadulterated surfaces, especially the floor, and the absence of any smoke ventilators or associated troughs. Bathgate was a typical example of the rebuilding programme instigated by BR to bring the steam locomotive sheds up a standard whereby maintenance and servicing could be carried out by staff in reasonable modern surrounding compared with the circumstances prevailing at most engine sheds at Nationalisation. In the event the somewhat gigantic plan to bring the depots into a semblance of modernity was an undertaking beyond the finances of BR. Dieselisation took place and the numerous steam sheds were no longer required, Bathgate passed into history. *F.W.Hampson.*

D34 GLEN LUSS, inside the rebuilt and, by now three-road shed, on Sunday 15th August 1954. Since its photograph of early 1953, it had been to Inverurie works for a Heavy General overhaul and repaint (10th July to 14th August 1953) which effectively got rid of the LNER on the tender sides. Its external condition one year after that works' visit leaves a lot to be desired. Transferring from St Margarets to Bathgate in October 1949, the 4-4-0 remained active until April 1961. Shortly afterwards another journey to Inverurie saw it broken up during the summer of 1961. *F.W.Hampson.*

Rebuilt, refurbished and re-clad on a number of occasions over the near sixty years of the depot's operation, the coaling stage appears to be in fine fettle on this Saturday afternoon in September 1960 with AWS equipped J37 No.64634 being tended to or, more than likely left to its own devices whilst the coalmen were down at the local pub. This particular 0-6-0 had transferred to Bathgate in April 1956 and stayed to withdrawal in January 1964. Considering places like Polmont were liberally stocked with these capable engines, Bathgate had less than a dozen allocated throughout the life of the class. The first examples did not arrive until December 1943 when three were transferred in but they left shortly after the ending of the war. In 1951 two others turned up, No.64601 in March and 64583 in June; the latter remained until withdrawn in December 1963 but the former had left by May 1953. No.64553 came in March 1952 and worked from Bathgate for the next ten years. Except for the above mentioned, no more came until January 1962 when Nos.64554 and 64569 arrived, both left in 1964. Two further members had a brief residency: No.64606 from February to November 1964 but holding the record for the shortest stay was No.64625 – 15th July to 26th August 1963!. *C.J.B.Sanderson.*

The completed shed on 5th April 1964 with one of the resident J36 holding centre-stage. The Fifties' remodelling of the shed had converted the original six roads into three running roads, with an attached one road repair facility on the north side of the building. The corrugated asbestos cladding used so profusely then would not be entertained in this day and age but in the Fifties' it was the medium to use for lightweight construction and to cut costs! Save for the spilt coal, note that the concrete pad is remarkably clean. The shed building was taken over for private use after closure and apparently survived into the 1990s as a workshop for a road haulage business. Inside the shed on this day in 1964 were a number of surprise occupants of which more will be revealed later but, those with exceptional eyesight might be able to spot them now. *C.J.B.Sanderson.*

So this is where the St Margarets allocated ex-LMS 'Dock Tank' ended up after being discarded but not yet condemned. The date is 4th October 1959 and No.47162 has joined others at this convenient storage/dump at Bathgate. Withdrawal was still a couple of months away but for how long it rotted here before being towed away for scrap is unknown. This was only the second member of the class to be withdrawn, No.47169 from Greenock's Ladyburn shed having the dubious honour of the being the first to succumb just three months beforehand. Lots more locomotives were to occupy this space at Bathgate in the years to follow, No.47162 simply started a 'trend' which would become an industry! *C.J.B.Sanderson.*

A3 No.60101 and others stored at Bathgate in April 1964. This Pacific had been lying derelict at 64F for some time and on 1st December last it was reported that the 'dump' here contained the following stored locomotives: A4 No.60023 (by 5th April 1964 this had been joined by Nos.60026 and 60034); A3 Nos.60057, 60087, 60089, 60098, 60099, 60101; A1 Nos.60159, 60161, 60162; A2 Nos.60529, 60534, 60537; V2 Nos.60892, 60965, 60969, 60971, 60980; 0-6-0s Nos.64612, 65224, 65251, 65290, 65344; others: Nos.68095, 68477, 69211 and Stanier Cl.5 Nos.45022 with 45023. The A4s mentioned were actually inside the shed, sheeted over and all three still carried their nameplates whereas the other Pacifics did not. Note that No.60101 was not amongst the A3s fitted with the so-called German type smoke deflectors. *F.Coulton.*

The nameplate of GOLDEN EAGLE is exposed for the photographer by shed staff at Bathgate when the tarpaulin sheet covering the front end of No.60023 was drawn back on 5th April 1964. Both 60023 and 60034 had virtually ended 1963 stored at Galashiels but in the final days of December they were hauled, independently, to Hawick shed from where they were prepared to make their own way to St Margarets shed for a short time in traffic. 1964 saw their arrival at Bathgate for a further period of storage. Of the Bathgate trio, all three were re-allocated to Ferryhill on 17th May 1964 where their fortunes varied; 60023 was the first to go in October of that year; 60026 lasted until December 1965 but was then slowly cannibalised at Crewe of all places to make another A4 worthy for preservation; 60034 worked the Glasgow expresses until August 1966 when it too was condemned! Another of the '64' group locomotive depots not normally associated with former LNER streamliners, the ex-Caley shed at Dalry Road, hosted two other stored A4s by the end of 1963 – Nos.60006 and 60007. Both of Dalry Road pair returned to traffic by mid-May 64' too. *F.Coulton.*

The dump in September 1962 had spread to the sidings immediately west of the engine shed. All sorts began to congregate the vintage didn't matter because Scottish Region was eager to rid itself of steam motive power as soon as possible. Amongst those on the dump were D11/2, J36, J39, J88, K3, N15, V1, V2, V3, Y9, etc. *A.Ives.*

64G HAWICK

A general view of the shed yard at Hawick 64G, on Saturday 21st July 1951 with activity centred around just four engines. Over at the passenger station a southbound passenger train waits in the Up platform. Up to the middle of October 1956, Hawick had a direct passenger service to Newcastle and any suitable motive power would be employed on those workings – 4-4-0, 2-6-0, 4-6-0. Any of the locomotives on view here, excepting the 0-6-0, could have been candidates for the Newcastle job. *C.J.B.Sanderson.*

Resident D30 No.62440 WANDERING WILLIE stables on the yard in September 1957 looking tired though actually only thirty-seven years old. Withdrawal was some ten months away in mid-July 1958. The D30 class had been allocated to Hawick since the late 1920s and by the mid-Fifties' eight of the class were resident at 64G. A visit to the shed on Saturday 13th October 1956 found the following motive power on shed: B1 No.61398, K3 Nos.61851, 61855, D30 Nos.62423, 62428, 62432, 62440, J35 No.64463, J36 Nos.65232, 65317, C16 No.67489, BR Cl.2 No.78047. Four of the depot's D30s were out working! *F.W.Hampson.*

This is the rear aspect of the engine shed prior to rebuilding. The date is 10th July 1950 and three of the shed's C16 Atlantic tank stud grace the yard in the late evening sunshine. Dating from 1849, the stone built shed appears to have new roof cladding in the shape of corrugated iron sheets. However, though this kind of mini-expenditure was deemed enough for many engine sheds on BR during that period, Hawick was to have its roof profile changed whereby the walls were raised and a shallower pitched roof replaced this post-war effort. Note that the water tank had not only been raised to a new elevation, level with the top pitch of the shed roof, but the tank had also been enlarged with additional plates being fixed along the top edge to more than double capacity. *C.J.B.Sanderson.*

A lull in the proceedings at Hawick on Monday evening, 16th September 1957 reveals a long gone tranquil scene which is now pure railway history. The passenger station is quiet whilst the only sounds at the engine shed are coming from a couple of visiting enthusiasts inspecting the simmering locomotive stud on the shed yard. Bells in the signal box will announce the next approaching train but once that has passed through, calm will once again return to this once important distant outpost of the erstwhile Waverley route. A couple of interesting pieces of passenger rolling stock complete the view. The Hawick coaling stage, and the turntable, was located some distance from the shed yard on the Down side of the main line, nearly five hundred yards north of this position. *C.J.B.Sanderson.*

No.78047 in July 1961. The Cl.2 is holding onto the merest semblance of a post-overhaul shine to its livery. Note the Scottish Region numerals now gracing the cab side – much larger than the original BR figures. This illustration affords a look at the south side of the engine shed after rebuilding, the wall extension being accomplished using bricks instead of local stone! Aesthetically it looks a mess but it is serving a purpose and for once somebody at BR had an eye on the future and the coming end for this 112 years old motive power depot. Note the original arched doorway has been retained with a nice set of wooden doors to finish off the job. Closure of Hawick engine shed took place on 15th January 1966! *N.W.Skinner.*

Although it may have often passed through hauling expresses, A3 No.60041 SALMON TROUT was never allocated to Hawick but on 12th April 1963 it paid a visit for reasons unknown. The Pacific is fairly clean and although it had undergone a General overhaul which had finished in January last, the cleanliness some three months after that event is uncanny. Based at St Margarets since transfer from Haymarket in July 1960, the big engine was possibly one of the strategically placed stand-by engines employed because the Royal train was traversing the Waverley route on this day. That explanation covers both reasons why an extraordinarily clean 64A A3 was at Hawick in 1963, and with a tender full of coal! *C.J.B.Sanderson.*

With the arched entrances consigned to history at this end of the shed, a rolled steel joist provides better clearances for locomotives and personnel though the restricted clearance sign affixed to the wooden staircase advises of some kind of restriction!. The date is 5th April 1964 and two of Hawick's resident Standard tender engines create a haze in the Sunday morning sunlight. Note the roof ventilator has been raised on one side to enable natural light to stream into what would otherwise be a dark, dingy, interior. Outside, the fitters' bench, along with its accompanying vice, add further interest to an assortment of springs, brake blocks, and fire irons. What appears to be an animal skin is tied and spread to the legs of the wooden stairway. Whatever that object was – more than likely a rug, curtain or a towel beyond saving – its chances of drying without a blemish would have been somewhat marred. At the other end of the shed the arched doorway was still in situ. *F.Coulton.*

At the beginning of July 1964 the allocation of Hawick shed was down to just five locomotives, all BR Standards; Nos.76049, 78047, 78048, 78049, and 80113. One of the Cl.2s stood as pilot whilst the Cl.4 tank worked the Carlisle passenger services on a regular basis. Cl.4 No.76049 usually had charge of the Jedburgh goods job, at least until the Roxburgh Junction-Jedburgh branch closed in early August 64'. On 15th July Cl.2 No.78048 was condemned and the allocation shrunk once again. Many of the through workings at Hawick were by this time diesel-hauled, the infamous 'Claytons' joining the 'Peaks' and EE Type 4s on passenger trains. However, steam power was still prevalent with V2s and all manner of ex-LMS types using the Waverley route – hence the requirement for the Cl.2 pilots at Hawick. The long-standing passenger express over the route, *THE WAVERLEY*, was discontinued at the end of the summer timetable, a three-car diesel multiple unit running in its place between Edinburgh and Carlisle – the end was certainly in sight. This is No.78048 lying forlorn at the rear of the engine shed on 22nd August 1964 after a four year association with Hawick depot – others had resided longer, 78047 for ten years, 78046 for nine. The shed itself still had nearly eighteen months life ahead of it but by then only diesel locomotives in the shape of Clayton Type 1s would grace the stabling roads. *A.Ives.*

64H LEITH CENTRAL

Have you ever seen a more grandiose engine shed? This is Leith Central (64H) on 1st October 1955 some three years after it ceased to be used as a passenger station. Opened in 1903 by the North British Railway, in the days when the private railway companies would spend (squander) vast amounts of money to thwart a rival organisation getting into an advantageous position, this was the result of Caledonian and NBR rivalry. The terminal station had four platforms on two islands but even that proved to be too much for the meagre traffic which frequented this edifice to stupidity. On 7th April 1952 British Railways closed the loss-making station but did not immediately demolish the place. By 1955 plans were drawn up to convert the train shed into an engine shed where, initially, multiple unit stock could be stabled and driver training carried out without too much affect on Edinburgh's local engine sheds. So, Leith Central (64H) was born. In this illustration, looking over the Easter Road bridge, activity concerning the demolition of the platforms and conversion of the track beds is taking place. Stanier Cl.5 No.44995 blows off beneath the great roof perhaps to frighten off the pigeon population which had thrived undisturbed although at this time empty carriage stock was still being stabled. *C.J.B.Sanderson.*

Less than two years later and on the penultimate day of August 1957 the transformation is complete. Edinburgh-Glasgow Inter-City d.m.us were taking advantage of the new facility. Diesel locomotives would come and go, some loaned, others actually allocated for short periods. English Electric Type 1 Bo-Bo D8006 was one of the first to use the shed here when, in October 1958, it was resident for a week or so whilst on a familiarisation tour of Scottish depots. BRC&W Type 2s D5320 and D5321 came direct from the makers on 18th April 1959 and after a month they dispersed to Haymarket. Next came the EE Type 1s again, this time three new ones: D8028, D8029 and D8030, direct from Vulcan Foundry in December 1959. They all moved on to Kittybrewster in early 1960 but their presence enabled Scottish Region drivers and fitters to master them. The heavyweight brigade was represented by two English Electric Type 4s, D253 and D254, which came from York in January 1960 and returned south during the following March. The last main line locomotive recorded as allocated to 64H was BR Sulzer Type 2 D5117 which arrived on 15th April 1961 and moved on to Inverness in June. Of course, diesel shunters galore in all shapes and sizes have graced this place over the years and continued to do so until 1972 when it was closed and once again allowed to become derelict until demolished in 1989. *C.J.B.Sanderson.*